# WHERE ARE THEY NOW?

**EXTINCT ANIMALS THAT ONCE WALKED THE EARTH**
**SCIENTIFIC EXPLORER THIRD GRADE | CHILDREN'S ZOOLOGY BOOKS**

BABY PROFESSOR
EDUCATION KIDS

First Edition, 2019

Published in the United States by Speedy Publishing LLC, 40 E Main Street, Newark, Delaware 19711 USA.

© 2019 Baby Professor Books, an imprint of Speedy Publishing LLC

Baby Professor Books are available at special discounts when purchased in bulk for industrial and sales-promotional use. For details contact our Special Sales Team at Speedy Publishing LLC, 40 E Main Street, Newark, Delaware 19711 USA. Telephone (888) 248-4521 Fax: (210) 519-4043. www.speedybookstore. com

10 9 8 7 6 * 5 4 3 2 1

Print Edition: 9781541949218
Digital Edition: 9781541951013

See the world in pictures. Build your knowledge in style.
https://www.speedypublishing.com/

# TABLE OF CONTENTS

In this book, we're going to talk about extinct animals, so let's get right to it!

During the course of Earth's history, there have been millions of species. In fact, scientists estimate that there are over 8.7 million species living on Earth today.

However, species sometimes go extinct as well. There are many reasons this happens. Sometimes it's a disastrous event such as an asteroid hitting the Earth. Sometimes it's just a gradual loss of their habitat or food source. There have even been times when scientists thought an animal was extinct only to find that there are a few such animals still alive.

# WHY DO ANIMALS GO EXTINCT?

Group of scientists working at the laboratory

Even though there are now millions of species on Earth, scientists believe that since life began, as many as 99.9% of the species that existed at one time have gone extinct. Here are some of the reasons why this happens and sometimes it's a combination of these reasons as well.

- Large asteroids hitting the Earth's surface, which causes extreme conditions

- An enormous change in the climate

- Infectious diseases

- Loss of habitat caused by natural events or because of human civilization

- Lack of genetic diversity, which simply means that there is a dwindling population so the species gets weaker

• There are competitive species around that have adapted to the environmental conditions better than they have

• An invasive species has taken over the land and their food sources so there isn't enough space or food to support their population

• Too much human-caused pollution has made their habitat toxic

• Overhunting by humans caused them to die out

Unfortunately, as soon as humans began to farm, about 10,000 years ago, our impact on Earth's environment has caused many different species to go extinct.

Primitive agriculture

# DINOSAURS ONCE ROAMED THE EARTH

Paleontologists have discovered more than 700 dinosaur species to date.

Archaeological and paleontological find of dinosaur fossil on stone

These amazing creatures, such as Tyrannosaurus rex, Brontosaurus, Triceratops, Stegosaurus, and Argentinosaurus, were huge animals that walked the Earth for about 180 million years.

Tyrannosaurus rex

Brontosaurus

Triceratops

Stegosaurus

Argentinosaurus

Then, about 66 million years ago, an enormous asteroid hit the Earth in the Yucatan Peninsula. Recent evidence shows that about 33,000 years after the asteroid hit, all the dinosaur species went extinct. It was a gradual process. The only dinosaurs that didn't go extinct were those that had already evolved into birds.

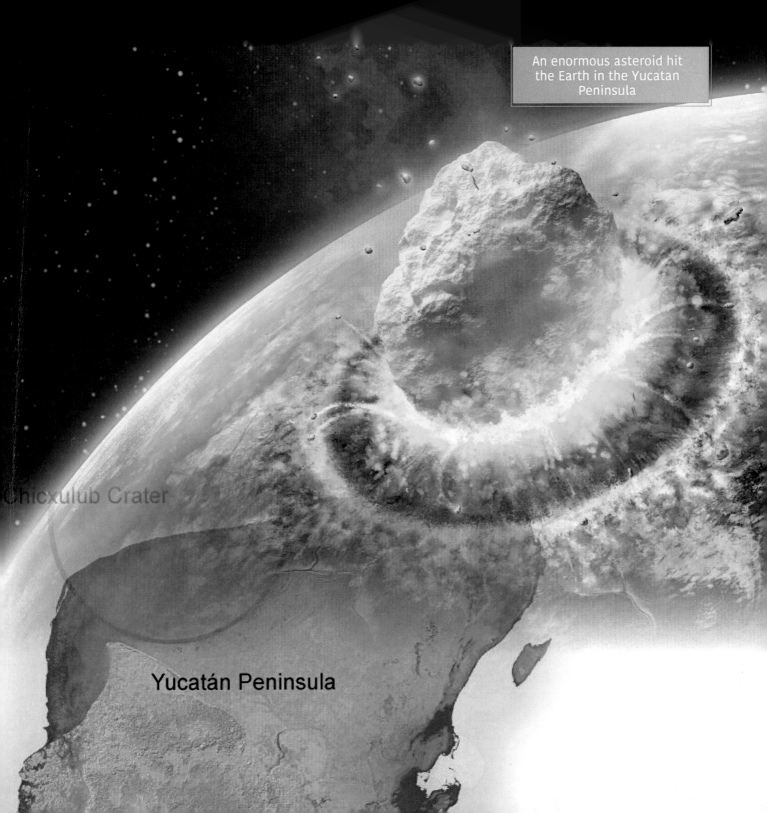

An enormous asteroid hit the Earth in the Yucatan Peninsula

Chicxulub Crater

Yucatán Peninsula

# WHY DID DINOSAURS GO EXTINCT?

Scientists have recently discovered that the populations of dinosaurs were already at risk before the asteroid hit.

Dinosaurs were already at risk before the asteroid hit the Earth

There were volcanoes in the region of present-day India that were causing havoc to the world's climate. Earlier asteroid strikes had more than likely weakened the environment as well. Human beings hadn't evolved yet when all of this occurred, so dinosaurs and human beings never existed on Earth at the same time.

Volcanoes in the region of present-day India that were causing havoc to the world's climate

# SMILODON

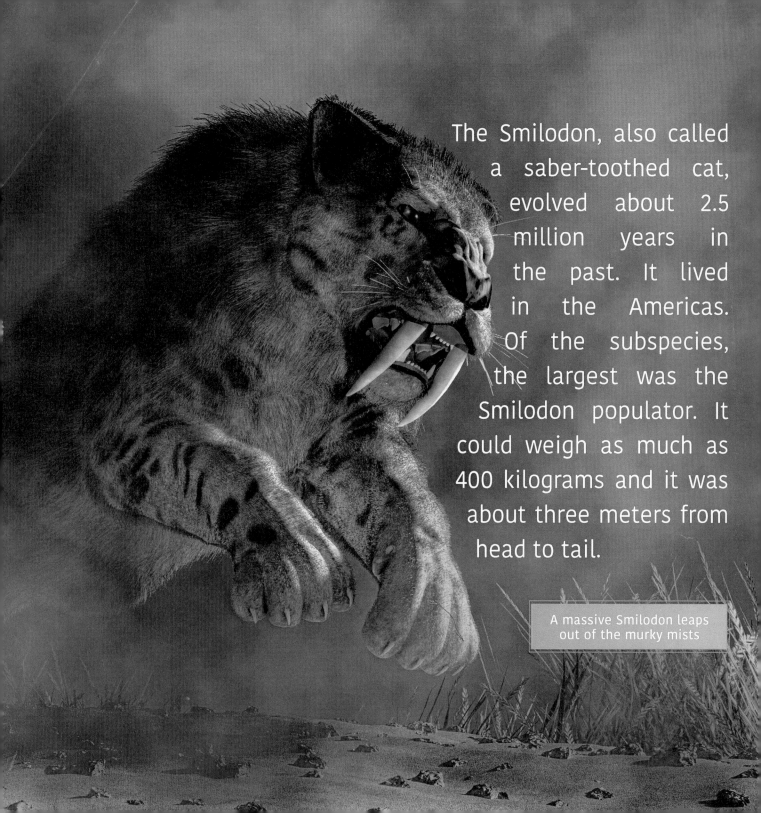

The Smilodon, also called a saber-toothed cat, evolved about 2.5 million years in the past. It lived in the Americas. Of the subspecies, the largest was the Smilodon populator. It could weigh as much as 400 kilograms and it was about three meters from head to tail.

A massive Smilodon leaps out of the murky mists

Its body had a structure that was similar to a bear instead of a tiger. Its limbs were short but powerful, though not suitable for running at high speed.

A Smilodon's body structure is similar to a bear

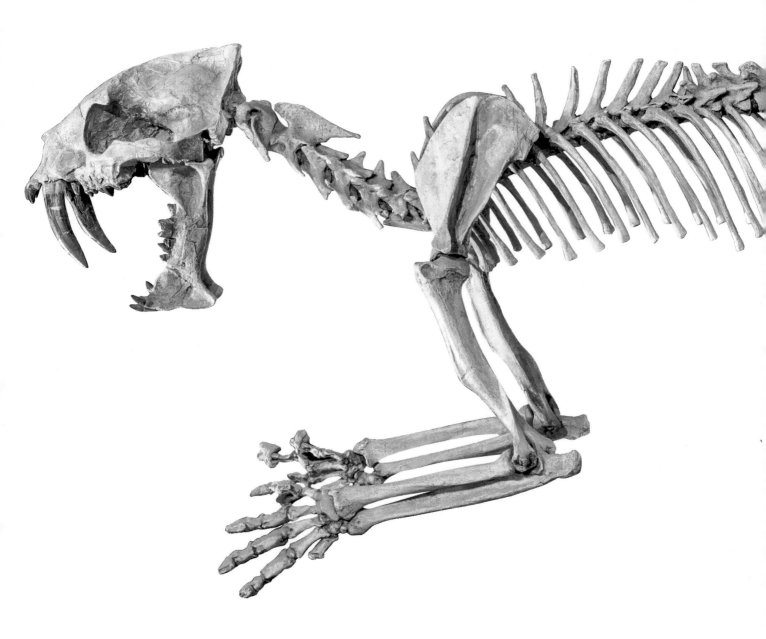

Its huge canine teeth could reach a 12-inch length, but they weren't strong and were mostly used after its prey was already injured. It could open its jaws very wide.

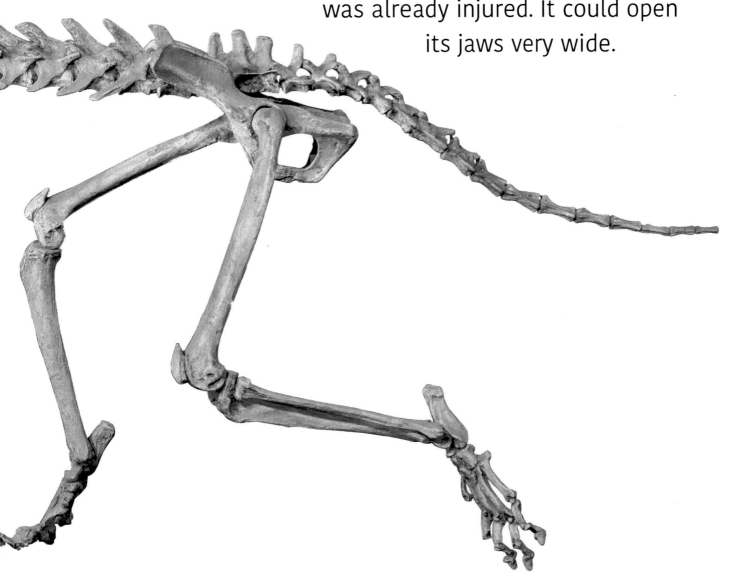

# WHY DID SMILODONS GO EXTINCT?

It's not known precisely why the Smilodon went extinct. Its diet consisted of deer, bison, and small-sized mammoths. It also ate dead animals. Smaller, faster prey could escape from its jaws.

A Smilodon attacking a deer

When humans arrived on the scene, they began hunting some of the species the Smilodons ate, so it's possible that the Smilodon couldn't hunt down enough food. It's believed that Smilodons went extinct about 10,000 B.C.

Caveman and Smilodon

# IRISH ELK

At one time, the giant Irish elk roamed from the country of Ireland to the frozen land of Siberia. They evolved about 400,000 years in the past. From ground to shoulder they were as tall as seven feet in height. They could weigh as much as 700 kilograms.

An Irish Elk, a breed of extinct pleistocene deer

They didn't have much in common with the species of elk alive today, but were more similar to today's deer. However, their antlers were enormous and could reach a width of 12 feet!

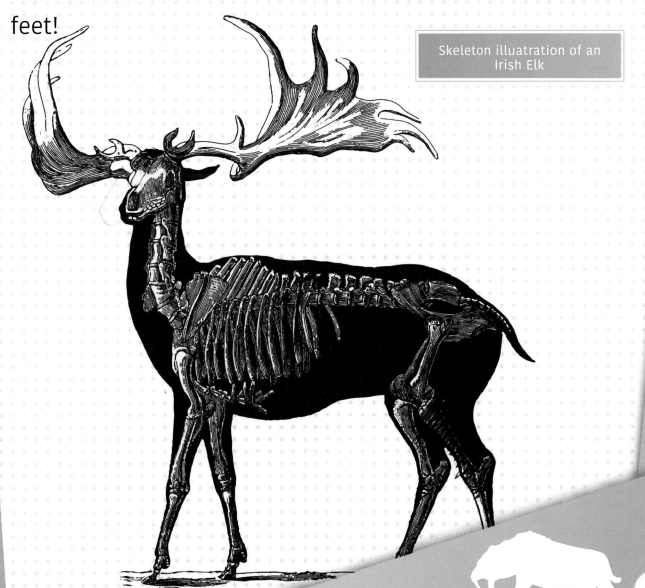

Skeleton illuatration of an Irish Elk

# WHY DID IRISH ELK GO EXTINCT?

Irish elk died out about 5,000 years ago. There may have been several factors that led to their extinction. Hunting by humans may have been one reason.

The scientific name of the Irish Elk is megaloceros

Also, at that time, the ice from the last glacial era was melting. Different plants began to cover the ground, which made it difficult for the elk to consume the minerals, particularly calcium, they needed to keep their antlers strong.

As the ice from the last glacial era started to melt, it became difficult for the elk to consume the minerals from the ground.

# WOOLLY MAMMOTH

Wolly Mammoths in the Arctic region

About 12,000 years ago, during the beginning of the Holocene epoch, woolly mammoths roamed the arctic regions of the Northern Hemisphere.

They were huge animals. They reached a maximum height of 11 feet. They were about the same size and weight as African elephants, although their DNA more closely resembled Asian elephants.

They had fur that ranged in color from brown to black to ginger. They also had short tails that were not susceptible to frostbite.

These prehistoric ice age mammals had fur that ranged in color from brown to black to ginger.

# WHY DID WOOLLY MAMMOTHS GO EXTINCT?

Scientists believe that there were two major reasons that the woolly mammoths went extinct. Humans hunted them for their tusks and their meat.

3d illustration of prehistoric men hunting a young mammoth

The second reason was the climate change. As the ice began to melt, their habitats began to decrease and their populations got smaller.

As the ice began to melt, their habitats began to decrease

Most of them <u>perished</u> about 10,000 years in the past, but there were a few populations that <u>remained alive</u> until 2000 <u>B.C.</u>, which was about 4,000 years ago.

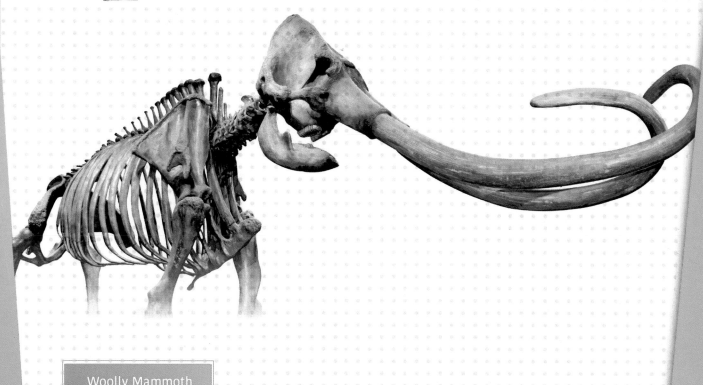

Woolly Mammoth
Skeleton

# MOA

The moa was a large bird that couldn't fly. These birds were native to the country of New Zealand. They were very tall and could grow to 12 feet in height. They weighed about 230 kilograms.

The Extinct Giant Moa

Even though they were very tall, the fossils found show that they spent much of their time with their necks bent down in front of them. Their long necks meant that they made low-pitched calls to communicate with each other.

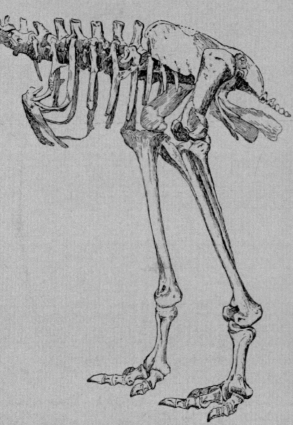

KOSTRA VYMŘELÉHO PTÁKA MOA

A skeleton of moa, an extinct bird of New Zealand

# WHY DID THE MOA GO EXTINCT?

Hunters in New Zealand killed the moas no matter whether they were adult birds or not. Scientists have determined that this overhunting made the populations of moas decrease. The birds couldn't find mates so they eventually died out around 1400 AD.

Hunters in New Zealand killed the moas no matter whether they were adult birds or not

# STELLER'S SEA COW

Have you ever seen a manatee? They are large sea mammals that have strange faces.

Young Manatee

Steller's Sea Cow was similar, but much larger in size, with a maximum size of 30 feet from snout to tail.

Steller Sea Cow

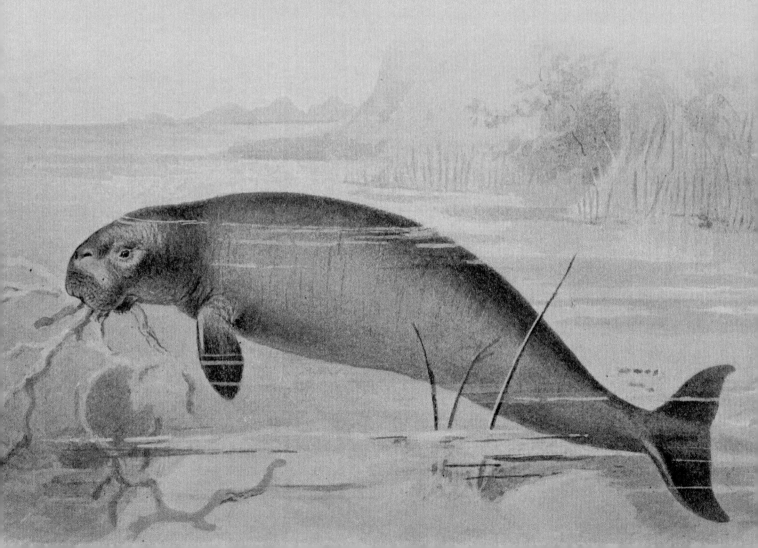

This animal was discovered and named for the zoologist Georg Wilhelm Steller. Unfortunately, once he discovered it, others followed his sea routes and hunted the animals into extinction within 30 years.

Georg Wilhelm Steller

Steller measuring a Steller Sea Cow

# WHY DID STELLER'S SEA COW GO EXTINCT?

Steller's Sea Cows would swim in shallow waters where they munched on reeds in the northern section of the Pacific Ocean.

Steller Sea Cow swimmming in shallow water

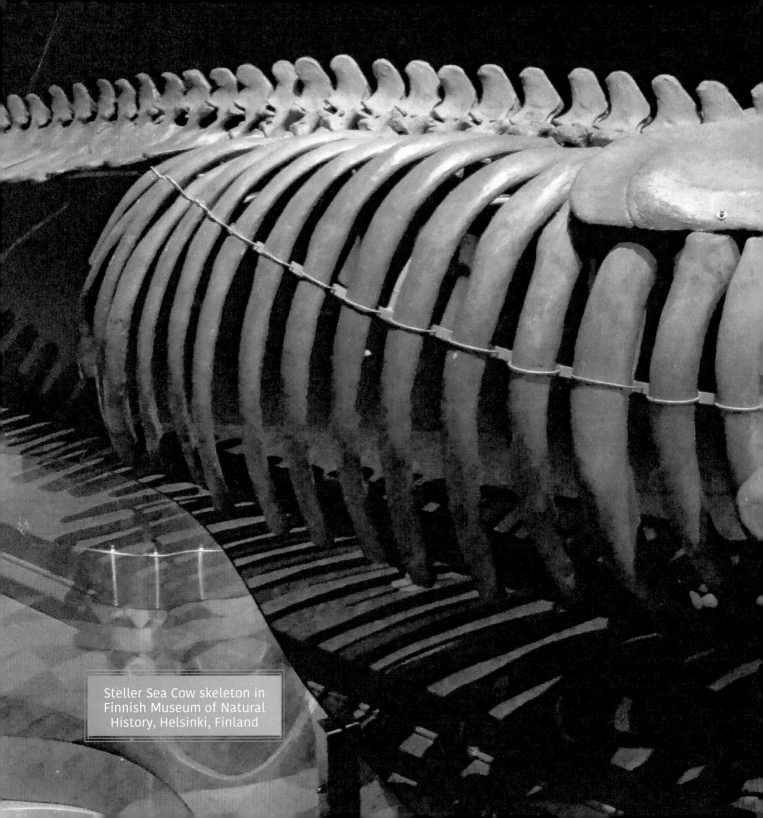

Steller Sea Cow skeleton in Finnish Museum of Natural History, Helsinki, Finland

Humans were more than likely responsible for their extinction around 1768 AD. They were hunted for meat and to make oil for lamps. Their skins were used to line the bottoms of boats to keep them free from leaks.

# GREAT AUK

Great Auk old illustration

Although it was a bird, the great auk couldn't fly. It was similar to the penguins we know of today.

It was a strong swimmer and stored fat reserves to stay warm like penguins as well. Its beak was heavy and hooked. Also like penguins, great auks mated and nested in dense colonies.

Great Auks in summer and winter plumage

2

Auks grew to a maximum height of three feet tall. Populations of auks lived in the northern section of the Atlantic Ocean.

Great Auk, specimen no. 77. Academy of Natural Sciences of Drexel University 1900 Benjamin Franklin Parkway Philadelphia

# WHY DID THE GREAT AUK GO EXTINCT?

Great Auks were killed by hunters

Beginning in the early 1500s, European hunters killed these birds to get their soft feathers to use in pillows. Later, North American hunters killed them to make fishing bait. Because they didn't fly, they were easy to catch.

As the species became rare, museums wanted to get specimens for their collections and this was the final blow that made the auks go extinct. They went extinct in 1852 AD.

Great Auk (Pinguinis impennis) specimen, Kelvingrove, Glasgow

The British government had tried to prevent the extinction from taking place. They passed an early environmental law in the 1770s to try to protect the birds from being killed, but sadly it was too little too late.

The Bristish government passed an environmental law in the 1770s to protect birds

# WILL SCIENTISTS BE ABLE TO BRING BACK EXTINCT ANIMALS?

Team of Medical Research Scientists Working

It may be possible in the future for scientists to bring back some animals that are extinct today.

For example, they may be able to bring back a hybrid of the woolly mammoth by using their DNA in combination with the DNA of modern-day Asian elephants. In order to determine whether an extinct species is a good candidate for a de-extinction or "comeback," scientists will need to decide whether:

- The species is desirable.
- The species helps the ecology.
- Humans want the species to undergo de-extinction.
- There is enough tissue to provide DNA samples that are usable.
- There are enough habitats and food for the animals to survive and that they will have limited contact with people.

circa

A concept of Wolly mammoth and Asian elephant DNA

Jurassic Park Movie

The Jurassic Park movies have shown the consequences of "rebirthing" dinosaurs, but there is little chance of that happening since dinosaurs don't score well on the items listed above. So, for the time being, dinosaurs aren't scheduled for a de-extinction.

# SUMMARY

Throughout the history of life on Earth many millions of species have gone extinct. To go extinct means that there are no living specimens of the animal left on Earth. We may never know about some animals that have gone extinct. The fossil records that scientists have found provide evidence for many others so we know of their existence even if they lived before humans walked on Earth. Ever since humans began to farm, many more animals have gone extinct due to loss of habitat and pollution. However, these are not the only reasons that animals go extinct. Natural disasters and climate change, whether it's influenced by humans or not, can cause animals to have dwindling populations and then go extinct.

Now that you've learned some facts about extinct animals, you may want to read more about dinosaurs in the Baby Professor book, *Dinosaur Facts for Kids - Animal Book for Kids | Children's Animal Books.*

Visit

www.BabyProfessorBooks.com
to download Free Baby Professor eBooks
and view our catalog of new and exciting
Children's Books

Made in United States
North Haven, CT
02 March 2022

16680469R10042